The Case For Democratic Socialism: A Thorough Analysis

Pierre Schuman

Copyright © 2019 Pierre Schuman

All rights reserved.

ISBN: 9781670180568

To all my fellow Americans, this work is dedicated to you. May this work keep you wise and vigilant against empty promises and false prophets.

CONTENTS

PREFACE

A new generation of woke peeps are being inspired to change our American ways and to embrace democratic socialism. Let's take a close look at its merits.

CHAPTER 1: PRINCIPLES

There is no case. It's basically just socialism. And socialism sort of sucks.

There is no case. It's basically just socialism. And
socialism sort of sucks.

There is no case. It's basically just socialism. And socialism sort of sucks.

There is no case. It's basically just socialism. And socialism sort of sucks.

There is no case. It's basically just socialism. And socialism sort of sucks.

There is no case. It's basically just socialism. And
socialism sort of sucks.

There is no case. It's basically just socialism. And socialism sort of sucks.

There is no case. It's basically just socialism. And socialism sort of sucks.

There is no case. It's basically just socialism. And socialism sort of sucks.

There is no case. It's basically just socialism. And socialism sort of sucks.

There is no case. It's basically just socialism. And
socialism sort of sucks.

There is no case. It's basically just socialism. And socialism sort of sucks.

There is no case. It's basically just socialism. And socialism sort of sucks.

There is no case. It's basically just socialism. And socialism sort of sucks.

There is no case. It's basically just socialism. And socialism sort of sucks.

There is no case. It's basically just socialism. And socialism sort of sucks.

There is no case. It's basically just socialism. And socialism sort of sucks.

There is no case. It's basically just socialism. And socialism sort of sucks.

There is no case. It's basically just socialism. And socialism sort of sucks.

There is no case. It's basically just socialism. And socialism sort of sucks.

There is no case. It's basically just socialism. And
socialism sort of sucks.

There is no case. It's basically just socialism. And socialism sort of sucks.

There is no case. It's basically just socialism. And socialism sort of sucks.

There is no case. It's basically just socialism. And socialism sort of sucks.

There is no case. It's basically just socialism. And socialism sort of sucks.

CHAPTER 2: ECONOMICS

There is no case. It's basically just socialism. And socialism sort of sucks.

There is no case. It's basically just socialism. And socialism sort of sucks.

There is no case. It's basically just socialism. And
socialism sort of sucks.

There is no case. It's basically just socialism. And socialism sort of sucks.

There is no case. It's basically just socialism. And socialism sort of sucks.

There is no case. It's basically just socialism. And socialism sort of sucks.

There is no case. It's basically just socialism. And socialism sort of sucks.

There is no case. It's basically just socialism. And socialism sort of sucks.

There is no case. It's basically just socialism. And socialism sort of sucks.

There is no case. It's basically just socialism. And socialism sort of sucks.

There is no case. It's basically just socialism. And
socialism sort of sucks.

There is no case. It's basically just socialism. And socialism sort of sucks.

There is no case. It's basically just socialism. And socialism sort of sucks.

There is no case. It's basically just socialism. And socialism sort of sucks.

There is no case. It's basically just socialism. And socialism sort of sucks.

There is no case. It's basically just socialism. And socialism sort of sucks.

There is no case. It's basically just socialism. And socialism sort of sucks.

There is no case. It's basically just socialism. And socialism sort of sucks.

There is no case. It's basically just socialism. And socialism sort of sucks.

There is no case. It's basically just socialism. And
socialism sort of sucks.

There is no case. It's basically just socialism. And
socialism sort of sucks.

There is no case. It's basically just socialism. And socialism sort of sucks.

There is no case. It's basically just socialism. And socialism sort of sucks.

There is no case. It's basically just socialism. And socialism sort of sucks.

There is no case. It's basically just socialism. And socialism sort of sucks.

CHAPTER 3: LABOR

There is no case. It's basically just socialism. And socialism sort of sucks.

There is no case. It's basically just socialism. And socialism sort of sucks.

There is no case. It's basically just socialism. And socialism sort of sucks.

There is no case. It's basically just socialism. And socialism sort of sucks.

There is no case. It's basically just socialism. And socialism sort of sucks.

There is no case. It's basically just socialism. And socialism sort of sucks.

There is no case. It's basically just socialism. And socialism sort of sucks.

There is no case. It's basically just socialism. And socialism sort of sucks.

There is no case. It's basically just socialism. And socialism sort of sucks.

There is no case. It's basically just socialism. And socialism sort of sucks.

There is no case. It's basically just socialism. And socialism sort of sucks.

There is no case. It's basically just socialism. And socialism sort of sucks.

There is no case. It's basically just socialism. And socialism sort of sucks.

There is no case. It's basically just socialism. And socialism sort of sucks.

There is no case. It's basically just socialism. And socialism sort of sucks.

CHAPTER 4: FOREIGN POLICY

There is no case. It's basically just socialism. And socialism sort of sucks.

There is no case. It's basically just socialism. And socialism sort of sucks.

There is no case. It's basically just socialism. And socialism sort of sucks.

There is no case. It's basically just socialism. And socialism sort of sucks.

There is no case. It's basically just socialism. And socialism sort of sucks.

There is no case. It's basically just socialism. And socialism sort of sucks.

There is no case. It's basically just socialism. And
socialism sort of sucks.

There is no case. It's basically just socialism. And
socialism sort of sucks.

There is no case. It's basically just socialism. And socialism sort of sucks.

There is no case. It's basically just socialism. And socialism sort of sucks.

There is no case. It's basically just socialism. And socialism sort of sucks.

There is no case. It's basically just socialism. And socialism sort of sucks.

There is no case. It's basically just socialism. And socialism sort of sucks.

There is no case. It's basically just socialism. And socialism sort of sucks.

There is no case. It's basically just socialism. And socialism sort of sucks.

There is no case. It's basically just socialism. And socialism sort of sucks.

There is no case. It's basically just socialism. And socialism sort of sucks.

There is no case. It's basically just socialism. And socialism sort of sucks.

There is no case. It's basically just socialism. And socialism sort of sucks.

There is no case. It's basically just socialism. And
socialism sort of sucks.

There is no case. It's basically just socialism. And socialism sort of sucks.

There is no case. It's basically just socialism. And socialism sort of sucks.

There is no case. It's basically just socialism. And
socialism sort of sucks.

There is no case. It's basically just socialism. And socialism sort of sucks.

There is no case. It's basically just socialism. And socialism sort of sucks.

There is no case. It's basically just socialism. And socialism sort of sucks.

CHAPTER 5: CULTURAL

There is no case. It's basically just socialism. And socialism sort of sucks.

There is no case. It's basically just socialism. And socialism sort of sucks.

There is no case. It's basically just socialism. And socialism sort of sucks.

There is no case. It's basically just socialism. And socialism sort of sucks.

There is no case. It's basically just socialism. And socialism sort of sucks.

There is no case. It's basically just socialism. And socialism sort of sucks.

There is no case. It's basically just socialism. And socialism sort of sucks.

There is no case. It's basically just socialism. And socialism sort of sucks.

There is no case. It's basically just socialism. And socialism sort of sucks.

There is no case. It's basically just socialism. And
socialism sort of sucks.

There is no case. It's basically just socialism. And socialism sort of sucks.

There is no case. It's basically just socialism. And socialism sort of sucks.

There is no case. It's basically just socialism. And socialism sort of sucks.

There is no case. It's basically just socialism. And socialism sort of sucks.

There is no case. It's basically just socialism. And socialism sort of sucks.

There is no case. It's basically just socialism. And socialism sort of sucks.

There is no case. It's basically just socialism. And socialism sort of sucks.

There is no case. It's basically just socialism. And socialism sort of sucks.

There is no case. It's basically just socialism. And socialism sort of sucks.

There is no case. It's basically just socialism. And socialism sort of sucks.

There is no case. It's basically just socialism. And socialism sort of sucks.

There is no case. It's basically just socialism. And socialism sort of sucks.

There is no case. It's basically just socialism. And socialism sort of sucks.

There is no case. It's basically just socialism. And socialism sort of sucks.

There is no case. It's basically just socialism. And socialism sort of sucks.

There is no case. It's basically just socialism. And socialism sort of sucks.

There is no case. It's basically just socialism. And socialism sort of sucks.

There is no case. It's basically just socialism. And
socialism sort of sucks.

There is no case. It's basically just socialism. And socialism sort of sucks.

There is no case. It's basically just socialism. And socialism sort of sucks.

There is no case. It's basically just socialism. And socialism sort of sucks.

There is no case. It's basically just socialism. And socialism sort of sucks.

There is no case. It's basically just socialism. And socialism sort of sucks.

There is no case. It's basically just socialism. And socialism sort of sucks.

There is no case. It's basically just socialism. And socialism sort of sucks.

There is no case. It's basically just socialism. And socialism sort of sucks.

There is no case. It's basically just socialism. And socialism sort of sucks.

There is no case. It's basically just socialism. And
socialism sort of sucks.

There is no case. It's basically just socialism. And socialism sort of sucks.

There is no case. It's basically just socialism. And socialism sort of sucks.

There is no case. It's basically just socialism. And
socialism sort of sucks.

There is no case. It's basically just socialism. And socialism sort of sucks.

There is no case. It's basically just socialism. And socialism sort of sucks.

There is no case. It's basically just socialism. And socialism sort of sucks.

There is no case. It's basically just socialism. And socialism sort of sucks.

There is no case. It's basically just socialism. And socialism sort of sucks.

CHAPTER 6: RACE

There is no case. It's basically just socialism. And socialism sort of sucks.

There is no case. It's basically just socialism. And socialism sort of sucks.

There is no case. It's basically just socialism. And socialism sort of sucks.

There is no case. It's basically just socialism. And socialism sort of sucks.

There is no case. It's basically just socialism. And socialism sort of sucks.

There is no case. It's basically just socialism. And socialism sort of sucks.

There is no case. It's basically just socialism. And
socialism sort of sucks.

There is no case. It's basically just socialism. And socialism sort of sucks.

There is no case. It's basically just socialism. And socialism sort of sucks.

There is no case. It's basically just socialism. And socialism sort of sucks.

There is no case. It's basically just socialism. And socialism sort of sucks.

There is no case. It's basically just socialism. And socialism sort of sucks.

There is no case. It's basically just socialism. And socialism sort of sucks.

There is no case. It's basically just socialism. And
socialism sort of sucks.

There is no case. It's basically just socialism. And socialism sort of sucks.

There is no case. It's basically just socialism. And socialism sort of sucks.

There is no case. It's basically just socialism. And socialism sort of sucks.

There is no case. It's basically just socialism. And socialism sort of sucks.

There is no case. It's basically just socialism. And socialism sort of sucks.

There is no case. It's basically just socialism. And socialism sort of sucks.

There is no case. It's basically just socialism. And
socialism sort of sucks.

There is no case. It's basically just socialism. And socialism sort of sucks.

There is no case. It's basically just socialism. And socialism sort of sucks.

There is no case. It's basically just socialism. And socialism sort of sucks.

There is no case. It's basically just socialism. And socialism sort of sucks.

CHAPTER 7: ENERGY AND CLIMATE CHANGE

There is no case. It's basically just socialism. And socialism sort of sucks.

There is no case. It's basically just socialism. And socialism sort of sucks.

There is no case. It's basically just socialism. And socialism sort of sucks.

There is no case. It's basically just socialism. And socialism sort of sucks.

There is no case. It's basically just socialism. And socialism sort of sucks.

There is no case. It's basically just socialism. And socialism sort of sucks.

There is no case. It's basically just socialism. And socialism sort of sucks.

There is no case. It's basically just socialism. And
socialism sort of sucks.

There is no case. It's basically just socialism. And socialism sort of sucks.

There is no case. It's basically just socialism. And socialism sort of sucks.

There is no case. It's basically just socialism. And socialism sort of sucks.

There is no case. It's basically just socialism. And socialism sort of sucks.

There is no case. It's basically just socialism. And socialism sort of sucks.

There is no case. It's basically just socialism. And socialism sort of sucks.

There is no case. It's basically just socialism. And socialism sort of sucks.

There is no case. It's basically just socialism. And socialism sort of sucks.

There is no case. It's basically just socialism. And socialism sort of sucks.

There is no case. It's basically just socialism. And socialism sort of sucks.

There is no case. It's basically just socialism. And
socialism sort of sucks.

There is no case. It's basically just socialism. And socialism sort of sucks.

There is no case. It's basically just socialism. And socialism sort of sucks.

There is no case. It's basically just socialism. And socialism sort of sucks.

There is no case. It's basically just socialism. And
socialism sort of sucks.

There is no case. It's basically just socialism. And socialism sort of sucks.

There is no case. It's basically just socialism. And socialism sort of sucks.

There is no case. It's basically just socialism. And
socialism sort of sucks.

CHAPTER 8: CRIME

There is no case. It's basically just socialism. And socialism sort of sucks.

There is no case. It's basically just socialism. And socialism sort of sucks.

There is no case. It's basically just socialism. And socialism sort of sucks.

There is no case. It's basically just socialism. And socialism sort of sucks.

There is no case. It's basically just socialism. And socialism sort of sucks.

There is no case. It's basically just socialism. And socialism sort of sucks.

There is no case. It's basically just socialism. And socialism sort of sucks.

There is no case. It's basically just socialism. And socialism sort of sucks.

There is no case. It's basically just socialism. And socialism sort of sucks.

There is no case. It's basically just socialism. And
socialism sort of sucks.

There is no case. It's basically just socialism. And socialism sort of sucks.

There is no case. It's basically just socialism. And socialism sort of sucks.

There is no case. It's basically just socialism. And
socialism sort of sucks.

There is no case. It's basically just socialism. And socialism sort of sucks.

There is no case. It's basically just socialism. And socialism sort of sucks.

There is no case. It's basically just socialism. And socialism sort of sucks.

There is no case. It's basically just socialism. And socialism sort of sucks.

There is no case. It's basically just socialism. And socialism sort of sucks.

There is no case. It's basically just socialism. And socialism sort of sucks.

There is no case. It's basically just socialism. And socialism sort of sucks.

There is no case. It's basically just socialism. And socialism sort of sucks.

There is no case. It's basically just socialism. And socialism sort of sucks.

There is no case. It's basically just socialism. And socialism sort of sucks.

There is no case. It's basically just socialism. And socialism sort of sucks.

There is no case. It's basically just socialism. And socialism sort of sucks.

There is no case. It's basically just socialism. And socialism sort of sucks.

There is no case. It's basically just socialism. And socialism sort of sucks.

There is no case. It's basically just socialism. And socialism sort of sucks.

There is no case. It's basically just socialism. And socialism sort of sucks.

There is no case. It's basically just socialism. And socialism sort of sucks.

There is no case. It's basically just socialism. And socialism sort of sucks.

There is no case. It's basically just socialism. And socialism sort of sucks.

There is no case. It's basically just socialism. And socialism sort of sucks.

There is no case. It's basically just socialism. And
socialism sort of sucks.

There is no case. It's basically just socialism. And socialism sort of sucks.

CHAPTER 9: IMMIGRATION

There is no case. It's basically just socialism. And socialism sort of sucks.

There is no case. It's basically just socialism. And socialism sort of sucks.

There is no case. It's basically just socialism. And socialism sort of sucks.

There is no case. It's basically just socialism. And socialism sort of sucks.

There is no case. It's basically just socialism. And socialism sort of sucks.

There is no case. It's basically just socialism. And socialism sort of sucks.

There is no case. It's basically just socialism. And socialism sort of sucks.

There is no case. It's basically just socialism. And socialism sort of sucks.

There is no case. It's basically just socialism. And socialism sort of sucks.

There is no case. It's basically just socialism. And socialism sort of sucks.

There is no case. It's basically just socialism. And socialism sort of sucks.

There is no case. It's basically just socialism. And socialism sort of sucks.

There is no case. It's basically just socialism. And socialism sort of sucks.

There is no case. It's basically just socialism. And socialism sort of sucks.

There is no case. It's basically just socialism. And socialism sort of sucks.

There is no case. It's basically just socialism. And socialism sort of sucks.

There is no case. It's basically just socialism. And socialism sort of sucks.

There is no case. It's basically just socialism. And socialism sort of sucks.

There is no case. It's basically just socialism. And socialism sort of sucks.

There is no case. It's basically just socialism. And socialism sort of sucks.

There is no case. It's basically just socialism. And socialism sort of sucks.

There is no case. It's basically just socialism. And socialism sort of sucks.

There is no case. It's basically just socialism. And socialism sort of sucks.

There is no case. It's basically just socialism. And socialism sort of sucks.

There is no case. It's basically just socialism. And socialism sort of sucks.

There is no case. It's basically just socialism. And socialism sort of sucks.

There is no case. It's basically just socialism. And socialism sort of sucks.

There is no case. It's basically just socialism. And socialism sort of sucks.

There is no case. It's basically just socialism. And socialism sort of sucks.

There is no case. It's basically just socialism. And socialism sort of sucks.

There is no case. It's basically just socialism. And socialism sort of sucks.

There is no case. It's basically just socialism. And
socialism sort of sucks.

There is no case. It's basically just socialism. And
socialism sort of sucks.

There is no case. It's basically just socialism. And socialism sort of sucks.

There is no case. It's basically just socialism. And socialism sort of sucks.

There is no case. It's basically just socialism. And socialism sort of sucks.

CHAPTER 10: TECHNOLOGY

There is no case. It's basically just socialism. And socialism sort of sucks.

There is no case. It's basically just socialism. And socialism sort of sucks.

There is no case. It's basically just socialism. And socialism sort of sucks.

There is no case. It's basically just socialism. And socialism sort of sucks.

There is no case. It's basically just socialism. And
socialism sort of sucks.

There is no case. It's basically just socialism. And socialism sort of sucks.

There is no case. It's basically just socialism. And socialism sort of sucks.

There is no case. It's basically just socialism. And socialism sort of sucks.

CONCLUSION: THE CASE FOR DEMOCRATIC SOCIALISM

There is no case. It's basically just socialism. And socialism sort of sucks.

ABOUT THE AUTHOR

Pierre Schuman holds a Bachelor of Arts in economics. His interests include international economic policy, the role of NGOs in the developing world, and contemporary cultural shifts in the United States.

www.ingramcontent.com/pod-product-compliance
Lightning Source LLC
Chambersburg PA
CBHW031053250726

48655CB00004B/1416